IT WORKED FOR US

BRITTANY & JEREMY KELLEM

www.TrueVinePublishing.org

It Worked for Us
Brittany & Jeremy Kellem

Published by True Vine Publishing Co. LLC
P.O. Box 22448
Nashville, TN 37202
www.TrueVinePublishing.org

ISBN: 978-1-956469-35-6: Paperback
ISBN: 978-1-956469-36-3: eBook

Cover by Brittany Kellem

Printed in United States of America

TABLE OF CONTENTS

WHERE WE ARE NOW

On this beautiful March Monday afternoon, we sit in our house with our two kids, having been together for 11 years and quickly approaching our sixth wedding anniversary. We are full of gratitude and appreciation towards God for all He has blessed us with. Things aren't perfect and we know they never will be, but things have gotten better for us and we believe they will continue to get better by the Grace of God.

There were times when we did not know if we would ever sit in our own house. There have been doctors who stated that they didn't believe we would have kids, but here we are. If you follow us on social media and see the pictures and videos we share, it may lead some to think that we have the ideal life. We will admit that we are blessed, but so are you. Everything is truly about perspective. We are firm believers that it is extremely important to have outer victories and private struggles. Meaning, we are quick to share our victories, but we are slow and very selective when disclosing our struggles. However, we both knew that one day we wanted to share our dating story and the struggles and the truths that people did not know or see from the outside. We have worked on this book for years. We have picked it up and placed it down numerous times. There were times we took weeks off from writing and there were times we got on a roll, but one thing we did know is that we needed to complete this book. We believe that this is a book that God has placed in us to write together. We believe that writing a book together truly strengthened our marriage and communication skills. It was not always easy. We were trying to take two minds and merge them to write a book. There were different details about the book that God placed in both of us, which required us to have to receive each other's input and work as a team to cohesively place it in a book.

This book is not your average book. This book is our story. This book is our Love Story. This book is our journey of waiting and dating until we said, "I do." We pray that you enjoy this book but more importantly, we pray that God uses this book to bless you and your life. We want to say thank you in advance for choosing to read our book. Enjoy!!

A MESSAGE FROM THE KELLEMS

Hey ladies, my husband and I have talked about doing this book together since we were dating in college. The number one question we got when we told people that we were waiting was, "How in the world are you two doing that?" We would always laugh it off and we always said that one day we were going to share with the world how we chose the road less traveled. The two of us met at the end of 2009 and by the beginning of 2010, he was officially bae. I wish we could tell you the road was easy, or that we never even thought about giving in, but it was quite the opposite! What I learned is that God really will keep those who want to be kept.

In this book, we keep it all the way real! There is no holding back, no sugar coating, but pure honesty. This book was not written to throw a bunch of scriptures at you, but to share with you our struggles, insecurities, and more than anything, how to submit your body to God as a living sacrifice. It is not that we wanted to put our whole dating experience in the eyes of the world, but to show you how two college students came together and said that we would strive to put God first in all that we say and do. We decided to practice abstinence, out of a commitment to God. Then once we began dating, we decided as a couple to wait. The struggle was all the way real and my desire is not for you to read this book and think that the two of us were perfect, but to strive to live a life where you don't continue in sin, so that grace should abound. We all sin and fall short. Although we can't live a sin-free life, we can strive to not continue in bondage and choose to sin less.

I know those who are reading this will all be at different stages in their lives. Some of you will say, "I have been waiting and just wanted a good read on how to continue to wait." Some of you will read this book and will have never considered waiting. That's okay too. This is a NO judgment zone. Others may find themselves like me, who truly want to wait but feel because they are no longer virgins that there is no point in waiting. The scripture tells us that when we see Jesus, He will tell us, "Well done." It does not say that He will say, "Well started," "Congrats, you never messed up," or "Great job that you never sinned." He will tell us, "Well done," which simply implies that it is not how you start, but how you finish.

Maybe you find yourself in the same situation that I was in years ago. You started right and then you made some poor decisions. Maybe you are just someone who wants to continue making the correct decisions and needs to know how to handle the various peer pressures. I hope this book will be a blessing to you, your besties, sisters, cousins, and friends! I pray my husband will be able to encourage young men, athletes, coaches, and males of all ages from the perspective of a man. May this book be an encouragement to you, that no matter what you have done up until this moment, God is faithful to forgive and present you as faultless. It is our hope that as we give you the male and female perspective, we are relatable to each of you.

Jeremy

What up fellas,

I know what you are thinking as you begin this book. You probably are asking yourself, "Why am I reading this book?" Some of you probably think you are weird for even entertaining a book suggesting waiting while dating. I must admit, I know the word wait normally does not appeal to us as human beings. Think about it. When we go to our favorite restaurant and we ask how long the wait is, and the host or hostess replies by saying 45 minutes, we begrudgingly walk away and decide to eat at another restaurant where there is no wait. What about when we are on a social media website and we click to watch a video, but it is taking a few more seconds than usual to load. Instead of waiting for the extra seconds to expire, we decide to exit the video and choose to watch something else. I'm guilty of doing this.

We are living in a world where choosing to wait for anything is becoming more of an anomaly. Nowadays, we can get information sent to our phones at the speed of light, which makes us humans dislike waiting for things. Not only are we becoming, as humans, allergic to the concept of waiting, but more specifically, as men we do not like the word "wait." Especially when it comes to dealing with women on a more intimate level.

If we are honest with ourselves, fellas, then we must confess that we have the propensity to want to go straight to home plate with the woman we are dating or have an interest in. We may not want to bunt for a single or even hit a double through the gap. Instead, we try to hit a homer on the first date, encounter, or within the first year of knowing a woman. We are notoriously known for not wanting to wait any length of time to get to know a woman in the most intimate way.

Therefore, being asked to wait until marriage is almost an absolute deal-breaker for a man. What I have come to realize, fellas, as I matured in my relationship with God, is that women are not the ones who are asking us to wait until marriage. The one who is asking and requiring us to do this is Jesus Christ. It took time for me to grasp this concept, but by the grace of God I did, and you can too.

Many of you guys have been lured into reading this book by your fiancé, girlfriend, or some type of lady friend in your life. On the other hand, there is a portion of you guys who are at a crossroad in your life. At this moment in your life, you are contemplating making pivotal decisions that specifically pertain to how you will conduct yourself moving forward in the relationship department. Trust me, fellas, I know where you sit.

There was a time when I did not want to stop fornicating. Even when I knew I should be waiting until marriage to have sex, it proved to be a momentous task to complete on my own. Some of you could be searching for answers or wanting to know if any other man has been through what you are experiencing. Whatever your reason for reading this book, just know my wife and I are glad you decided to read it. We will share our journey of waiting, hoping that our story will encourage you. We also believe our story will let you know that anything is possible with God, including waiting to partake in sex until you are married. I pray that God uses our book as a vessel to operate through, to bless your life and the lives of men and women across the world that read our book.

Love,

JK & Brittany

Matthew 25:21 (NIV): "His master replied, 'Well done, good and faithful servant! You have been faithful with a few things; I will put you in charge of many things.'"

CHAPTER 1

THE TRUTH

One of the most familiar stories in the Bible is the story of Adam and Eve. Just for refreshing purposes, in the beginning, God created a man and placed him in the Garden eastward of Eden. He then stated that it was not good for man to be alone and then created a woman. We know them by the names of Adam and Eve.

At that time, God had grown every tree that was good for food as well as the Tree of Life. In the Garden, God had grown the Tree of Knowledge, and it consisted of good and evil. God told them that they could eat from any tree, just not from the Tree of Knowledge. He informed them that if they did so, they would die.

One day, the enemy came to Eve in the form of a snake and began trying to convince her to eat from the Tree of Knowledge. Eve began telling the snake that she could not eat from the tree or they would die. The snake continued to tempt her and told her that if she was to go ahead and eat from the tree, she would become more like God. Eve went ahead and believed the lies from the snake and ate the fruit. Eve then gave Adam something to eat. The two of them then realized what they had done and were ashamed of their actions. As a result, they tried to go and hide from God.

We share this story as a reminder that we can attest that God has given us many things, but sometimes we desire that very thing He has asked us not to have. The thing with sex is not that God said we can't have sex, but He has asked that we wait until marriage. We as humans love wanting what we cannot have.

When you were younger, there may have been a time when your mom told you that you couldn't have a toy in the store. Minutes followed and you were either crying, sad, or throwing a tantrum. When you became a teenager, your mom may have told you that you couldn't go to the party because you needed to clean your room and as a result, the desire to go to the party became even greater.

What about the guy or girl who you pursued even though you knew they were not the right person for you, and on top of that they were already in a relationship? Has there ever been a time that you knew you should have waited before you made that large purchase, but you just couldn't help yourself and purchased it anyway? Why do we as humans crave forbidden fruit? The majority of the time it is not that God is saying you can't have it or will never have it, but He is saying, "I need you to wait!"

As humans, we all have our opinions about love, sex, intimacy, and what we should do with our bodies. In our own lives, we have discovered that there is only one legitimate source that has served us best when it comes to being a guideline for what we should do with our bodies. That source is the Bible. Now, we understand that you may not be a Christian or a reader of the Bible. Whatever stance you may have, we trust that the wisdom and knowledge that the Bible exudes concerning sex and our bodies

14

are beneficial for us all, if received and applied accurately in our lives.

In the scripture 1 Thessalonians 4:3-4, the Bible states, "For this is the will of God, your sanctification: that you abstain from sexual immorality; that each one of you knows how to control his own body in holiness and honor." We want you as you read this book to understand that it is not a woman or man that may be asking or prodding you to abstain from fornication or sexual immorality, but it is God who wants this from us all. Yes, we know that an actual person may be hinting to you that they desire to abstain from sex or may mention to you that you should wait until you are married before you partake in sex. You may indeed have friends who have decided to wait and are working to convince you to do the same because of the benefits they realize in their own lives and their dating relationship.

As a human, it is extremely difficult for us to disassociate the message from the messenger. Sometimes we choose not to take other people's suggestions. We say to ourselves that we do not have to listen to anyone else because we are adults, and we are too grown to take advice from others. We respect if that is your mindset but let us play angel's advocate. What if you looked at those people, whether it was your homegirl, homeboy, or significant other as being a conduit that God chose to convey His message through to you? It is God's will and preference that His people remain pure.

Some of you may be trying to figure out what good can come from starving yourself from sex. According to the scripture, those who choose to abstain from sexual immorality will in return know how to control their own body in holiness and honor. Abstinence teaches you self-control, especially in a physical way. There is no doubt that anyone who decides to refrain from sex faces an uphill challenge.

We can attest to that from personal experience. One thing we need you to know is that if you choose to abstain, the decision alone will not erase your desire for sex. The raging of hormones and the feeling of horniness will still be present in you, contrary to what you may think. Some people believe that those who are living a life of celibacy or abstaining from sex are immune to the sexual urges that exist in one who participates in sex regularly.

Unfortunately, it does not work like that. Hormones are not a switch that we can turn off and on depending on whether we are single or married. The same sex cravings that show up when you are sexually active never depart from you when the decision is made to practice abstinence. We know that telling you this may make you feel as if abstinence is an unconquerable task, but the good news is that as time passes, the more God will bless you with the knowledge and strength to control your body.

He equips you with the ability to deal with the urges of wanting to partake in sex without succumbing to the temptation. In 1 Corinthians 10:13, the Bible states, "No temptation has overtaken you except what is common to mankind. And God is faithful; he will not let you be tempted beyond what you can bear. But when you are tempted, he will also provide a way out so that you can endure it."

1 John 4:19 (NIV): "We love because He first loved us."

Brittany

CHAPTER 2

THE DECISION

As you begin developing a relationship with God, He will teach you the importance of waiting. As you read this book, we hope that you gain clarity on understanding the importance of waiting. My husband and I promised to share with you our past so that you know that we are relatable and we have sat exactly where you are sitting, faced the same peer pressure, and made many of the same mistakes. My background is that my mom and dad both are ministers, so I have spent my entire life labeled as a PK (Preachers' Kid).

The bar was set high and the standards were sometimes hard to meet. I remember when I was 16 years old, my mom was teaching a Bible study class on abstinence, and at that time, having premarital sex was the furthest thing from my mind. I hadn't been in a situation that I felt like I wanted to, nor had I been feeling the pressure in a relationship. I sat in the class and listened and wondered what was so hard about waiting. At that moment of time, I did not realize that I was going to soon experience the peer pressures of life and that what she was saying was going to be extremely beneficial for me to know.

I began what I called seriously dating later in my high school years and I started a campaign on encouraging young people to wait, titled "Are You a New Car or an Old Car?" The campaign started due to an assignment that was given to me by my teacher. I was going and speaking in places and telling young kids my age to wait until marriage. As the years went by, I became a hypocrite of my campaign.

I made the mistake and gave in to the decision of not waiting until marriage. Once I gave in, I felt my conscience constantly beat up on me. Although I was afraid of the consequences of my sin, I was more afraid to lose my relationship. Needless to say, over the next couple of years, I struggled with waiting or losing my relationship. There were so many red flags that God was trying to reveal to me, but, like many of us do, we ignore the signs until it hits us in the face. Over and over, I felt God telling me this wasn't the road that I should take, and that obedience was better than sacrifice. I would go to church and feel so convicted, but then turn around and make the same mistake. Over and over in my mind, I would tell myself what I was going to have to do. "But how?" was the exact question that ran through my mind.

I was exhausted from constantly living in bondage, but I was more afraid of being alone. My first year of college consisted of me talking to guys who I either talked to in high school or I was in the relationship that I found myself in that developed while I was working at my first job. I can honestly tell you that I learned so much from each of those relationships. I learned that sex will not keep a man, it will not make him treat you right, and it definitely will not keep him from cheating.

I began to wonder why I was sacrificing my body for sin. Why was I sacrificing my blessings for temporary moments? I knew those moments should have only been shared with my husband. I knew that I should have been more careful in protecting my gift; but instead, I felt as though I had been negligent. I cannot lie, I was extremely disappointed in myself.

One semester, I went to a camp with the Fellowship of Christian Athletes organization, and a lady was speaking. She was giving her testimony of how she waited to give her special gift to her husband. She was explaining to us how our bodies were temples and that they shouldn't be shared with anybody other than the man that God designed for us to marry. She didn't say anything that I didn't already know or had heard from my mom.

The difference was, I was so tired of sacrificing my happiness for hormones that can be controlled. As she spoke, tears ran down my face. She asked each of us in the section to bow our heads. She told us that she knew there were some young ladies in there that truly wanted to live a life that pleased God. She went on to say, "I know you are tired of being in bondage and I know you want to be set free."

With my head bowed, I thought, *How in the world does this lady know so much about my life?* I felt as though she was talking directly to me. I bowed my head and asked God for forgiveness like never before. I asked

20

Him to remove any guilt and help me stand on His word and His promises. I asked Him to help me move forward and make better decisions. I asked Him to save me. I knew I loved God so much, but I wasn't going to be able to save myself. I realized the only way that it was going to get better was for me to surrender my life to Him.

I was going to have to take a big step that was going to change everything as I knew it to be. I was going to have to leave camp and tell the guy that I was dating at the time that I wanted to practice abstinence. I was afraid of what his response would be, but I knew I couldn't change my decision. I ended up telling him that I wanted to wait and my prayer at the time was that he would wait too. I never got pregnant or had any unwanted diseases, but my conscience whooped me so bad.

I began telling him that I could no longer participate in premarital sex. I told him that I knew that God was telling me that He wanted more from me and that He was requiring more of me. God let me know He didn't just want me on Wednesdays at Bible study or church on Sundays. He wanted all of me! I don't think the guy I was dating took me seriously when I first told him. He later realized that I was determined to wait and that I was not changing my mind.

I didn't know what to think, but I knew what God told me I must do. I wondered if he was going to try to stick it out. Well, ladies, the exact opposite happened. I am not sure if you are familiar with the poet Ann Landers, but her poem was extremely relatable. She said, "I saw him, I liked him, I liked him, I let him, I let him, and guess what, he left."

That's exactly what happened—he left. The truth is, the two of us were not equally yoked in any area anyway, but I convinced myself that opposites attract. He didn't understand the point in waiting and he believed that the damage and the sin had already been done. On one hand, I felt bad that I had been living a double life and on the other hand, I was sad that I was letting go of a relationship that really should have never existed.

Over time, after a few mistakes and thoughts that I continued to have, I finally came to the complete decision to practice abstinence. I dreaded the thought of being single forever or having to tell the next person I met that I was waiting, in hopes that he wouldn't leave. In the back of my mind, I knew exactly what God was calling me to do. I remember praying to God, asking Him to send me a young man who loved Him as much as I did.

I prayed that I would meet a young man who would understand my worth and who was living a life where he would strive to put God first in all that he said and did. I realized that it wasn't going to completely be based on the man being committed to pleasing God alone, but I was going to have to be sold out for Jesus. As you read this book, you will continue to read our prayers, our mistakes, and our shortcomings, but you quickly find out that "to whom much is given, much is required."

Jeremy

Growing up as a child, my parents made it a priority to take me to church. Not only did I attend church, but I was also heavily involved in the church. I was an usher. I spoke the Word of God on the fourth Sunday of each month, which is when we would have our Youth Sunday service. I also sang in the choir.

I know what you are thinking. Can I sing? The answer is no, but you know how it is to be a member of a youth choir. It all sounds good as long as you are singing for the Lord. If you went to church as much as my family did then you would have heard hundreds of Bible verses. Many of the scriptures I adhered to, but some were not as simple for me to comply with.

In the Bible, it states in 1 Corinthians 6:18-20, "Flee from sexual immorality. Every other sin a person commits is outside the body, but the sexually immoral person sins against his own body." The verses continued, stating, "Or do you not know that your body is a temple of the Holy Spirit within you, whom you have from God? You are not your own, for you were bought at a price." The verse concludes with these words: "So glorify God in your body."

Many of us have heard this before or we can at least acknowledge that it is spiritually wrong to fornicate or partake in premarital sex. However, we decide to ignore this, as I did. I remember being a growing boy and becoming more intrigued by women. I started to notice their physical prowess and I began to feel a change inside as a maturing young man.

Once I was in high school, sex was a popular topic amongst my group of male high school friends. You were considered lame if you were not out on the prowl, attempting to sleep with as many girls as possible. I was not a guy that chased thousands of girls, but I must admit I was like your typical high school boy and chose to indulge in premarital sex. I knew it went against my faith as a Christian and a man of God.

At that time though, my flesh was stronger than my faith, in this particular area of my life. For years I struggled with sex. The Lord was number one in every other area of my life, but not this one. I could not let go. Once I got a taste of it, I could not imagine myself living without sex.

Especially being without it until marriage. There was no way I could hold out that long—at least, that's what I believed at that time. Consequently, I kept giving my body away, even though my body belonged to the Lord. Not only did it belong to the Lord, but my body belonged to my future wife, and at the time I had no clue of who she was going to be. I just knew God had one for me.

Fellas, you have to ask yourself this question: "Would I want my future wife to be engaging in sex with men who are not her husband?" I am sure your answer is no. Most men want the woman that they marry to have had as few sexual partners as possible prior to meeting them. If this is the case, don't you think women feel the same way?

In society, I know it is a double standard when it comes to the number of sexual partners a man can have compared to women. It is almost expected for a man to have a high number, but that does not have to be the case, and most women prefer you not. The choices I made regarding sex had to be answered for when I met my wife.

The uncomfortable dialogue took place between the two of us because of the irresponsible choices I made with my body. I wish I could have taken it all back, but that was impossible. I thought to myself, *Man, if I had only listened to God when He spoke to my conscience, warning me not to fornicate, and instead waited until I was married. Then all of this arguing and explaining would have been avoided.*

However, before meeting Brittany, I knew that I was supposed to be seeking God, being a blessing to others, and dating, but never crossing the sex barrier with any women. As a man of God, it was my responsibility to abstain, but I could not do it in my own strength. I needed the power and strength of the Lord to help me overcome this continual struggle. Like the building of Rome, it took time for me to get to the point of abstinence. It truly was a process—a process that consisted of failures and triumphs, and by the grace of God, I made it out stronger.

As was previously mentioned, my wife and I wanted to be vulnerable and transparent to the readers of our book. So, I will confess to you that I did not want to stop having premarital sex. My flesh wanted to continue to do so, but Jesus wanted me to stop. I knew there was a purpose and reason why He asks His people to wait until marriage. The world has made us believe sex is bad, but it cannot be. According to 1 Timothy 4:4, "For everything God created is good, and nothing is to be rejected if it is received with thanksgiving." That's including sex.

Sex is amazing when experienced in the correct context, and that context is between a man and woman who are married to each other. What makes having sex morally wrong is when it is done out of order. As humans, we tend to taint things when we choose to use them at an inappropriate time or in the wrong context.

For instance, sex is like a driver's license. Most people would agree that having a driver's license is not bad. However, if a driver's license is given to a ten-year-old kid, and it permits the kid to drive, then suddenly, the license becomes a bad thing, due to the age of the person who is using it. The context under which the license is used would lead us to think that the license is bad.

Therefore, realize sex is beautiful in God's eyes when done in covenant. Knowing all of this, I still did not want to quit indulging in sex, so I had to begin to pray and ask God to give me the strength to stop. I had to pray for strength to resist temptation and not put myself in situations wherein I would fail.

Now there were stumbling blocks along the way. I would like for you to believe that after praying, I then walked the straight and narrow from that point on and never partook in premarital sex again, but unfortunately, it did not go that way. There were slip-ups along the way to fully practicing abstinence until marriage. Like I previously stated, it was a process. It was like learning how to ride a bike without training wheels.

Before you were riding your bike with no help, or even when you made it to the point where you could take your hands off the handlebars or even pop wheelies, you fell off your bike a few times. Therefore, gentlemen, I need you to know that coming to the point where you are waiting until marriage takes time; you may fall down. Nevertheless, God is patient enough to work with you as He did with me.

God loves you so much, and He wants to see you giving great effort. He will also be there to pick you up every time you fall off the bike of abstinence. With that being said, I urge you to not abuse God's grace by continuing to fornicate just because you expect God to protect you from the consequences every time. By the grace of God, I was covered, but I knew that if I continued to fornicate, then I would increase the chances of me contracting an STD or even becoming a father before I was ready.

These are some of the results that you potentially draw near to incurring the more you dabble in fornication. On the contrary, I encourage you to inform God that you desire to refrain from sex until marriage, humble yourself, and then the Lord will assist you in getting to the point of living a lifestyle of abstinence. My sexual past could not be erased by the decision to abstain; nor can yours be.

What we are expected to do is move forward from our mistakes and ill-advised choices and live the life as single men that God has called us to live until we are married to the woman He has for us.

Luke 12:48 (NIV): "From everyone who has been given much, much will be demanded;"

Brittany

CHAPTER 3

OUR LOVE STORY

A t some point in your life, you get to the point of being tired of doing things your way and you begin realizing how much better it is to do things God's way. Have you ever been driving to a location and kept going to the wrong place? You finally decided to just turn on your GPS because clearly, you did not know the directions like you thought you did. That's the exact place that I had come to in life.

I realized that I was tired of going down dead ends, back ends, and cul-de-sacs, and I decided to seek God. I knew God was going to get me exactly where I needed to be. I was tired of being in meaningless relationships and trying to do things my way. I never was comfortable continuing in sin.

I honestly gave in because it seemed as if everyone around me was participating. I came to God and asked Him if He could design a man for me that loved Him with his whole heart. I confessed to Him that I wanted Him to send me someone who wasn't going to pressure me to do anything that didn't line up with His word. I asked God to send me someone that would choose to abstain instead of choosing to partake in premarital sex.

I knew that I was going to have to hold myself accountable and let the gentleman know up front that I was not sacrificing my body and that I was waiting until marriage. I wanted a man who loved God. I came to the realization that if a man doesn't love God, he cannot love me, because God is love. It is not that I was being unrealistic in what I wanted out of a man.

You may be wondering what kind of man I was looking for. Was I wanting him to not be attracted to me, or never have sinned a day in his life? No, I was very realistic about what I was wanting. I wanted a man that was attracted to me and even wanted sex. I just wanted the man God gave me to love God more than he loved me and in return, he would put God's desires first and his wants second.

Just in case you are wondering if God is still handing out the heart's desires, I wanted to briefly tell you my version of how Jeremy and I met. Like they say, "There are two versions to everything." In undergrad, I enjoyed going to a Bible study that was held by the Fellowship of Christian Athletes. Although I wasn't an athlete, I was a Christian and truly enjoyed going to Bible study. I had been introduced to the Bible study by my cousin while attending Tennessee State University (TSU).

After strengthening my relationship with Christ, I decided to transfer to another university. I left TSU and transferred to Middle Tennessee State University (MTSU). I wanted a change of scenery, and I knew I wanted a fresh start as I committed to being everything

God had called me to be. I arrived at MTSU still struggling with my decision to practice abstinence as well as other decisions. One of the hardest decisions you will ever make is daring to be different while being surrounded by peer pressure.

I began searching for a personal, deep relationship with God, not based on what my parents told me, but knowing God for myself. At times I would ask myself if it was that serious to wait or if fornication was a sin that God just excused. I know you are probably thinking that is crazy talk. You are so right!

I asked myself more of these questions because it seemed as if everyone had become comfortable with engaging in premarital sex, to the point I began questioning myself as to whether it was really that serious to wait. As my relationship with God grew immensely stronger, I learned that my body truly was a temple and that it was so important for me to decide to give God all of me.

So many times we want to choose what are major sins and what are minor sins. We want to say what are big lies and little lies, or if something is a huge mistake or a small mistake. I think we as humans label these things to make ourselves feel better when we do things that aren't right. We seem to always have an excuse and reason for our decisions. Although you never get to the point where you are free of sinning, it is still important to live a life where you choose to sin less every day. When you decide to die to yourself and live for Him, that's how you show God you are truly putting Him first.

When I arrived at MTSU, I decided to remove sense-less relationships. I was entertaining past relationships even though I knew the outcome. I decided it was impor-tant to show God I was completely surrendering. Since I had such a passion for attending the Fellowship of Chris-tian Athletes, I decided to visit the same organization at MTSU.

I had been invited by the leader of FCA on the cam-pus. I had met the leader at an FCA camp the year prior and had told him that I was going to come to visit. Little did I know at the time, I would be attending the school and later joining the organization on that campus. One Tuesday night, I arrived and there was Trevor the huddle leader, sitting on a cart. There wasn't anybody else in there and I wondered where everybody else could have been.

I sat down and approximately five minutes later, a young man named Jeremy Kellem (whose name I didn't know at the time) walked in and was eating a plate of food. He looked at me and asked me if I wanted any. I looked at him and said no. I had never seen or met him before, and I knew that I wasn't going to take food from him (lol). Now, I know I'm greedy, but not that greedy. So, Jeremy continued eating and the three of us had Bible study. I ended up traveling every Monday to the FCA at TSU and not attending MTSU's FCA again until the fol-lowing semester.

That next semester, I decided to go back to FCA on MTSU's campus. I heard the organization had grown and things were going well. I came and gave my testimony on how I came into abstinence and enjoyed the Bible study. While attending MTSU, I met a lady named Ms. Erica. She became a big sister and mentor to me. One night we were talking and I was telling her how I was practicing abstinence and how I was frightened by the idea that I was never going to find someone. She told me God was going to send me someone. We closed out the conversation and prayed. The next day she called me, saying she knew a young man that God had placed on her heart. She went on to say that he was in a Bible group on campus, but she couldn't remember the name. I said, "No ma'am, I do not let older people match me up." We laughed and ceased the conversation on the subject.

A week later, I walked into FCA, I sat down, and they told everyone to greet people around them. I remember Jeremy turning around and saying, "Hey, how have you been, I haven't seen you in a while." Immediately, I started crying. To this day I can't tell anyone why I started crying.

It's hilarious when we talk about it now. At the time, a lot of things were going through my mind. I thought to myself, *How on a campus this big could this be the person that my mentor was talking about?* What were the odds that I would have met him at FCA with it only being my second time seeing him?

Then I thought, *Could this be the person for me?* It is crazy! Well, needless to say, it scared Jeremy, because he assumed that I didn't like him and wasn't interested. He was able to put two and two together that I was who my mentor had mentioned to him too.

He went to her and told her, "I think the Brittany you know goes to FCA and I don't think Brittany likes me." He went on to tell her that I started crying as soon as he asked me how I was doing. Jeremy told my mentor that if I was interested, to tell me to text him. My mentor gave me the number and I texted Jeremy, "Hi," and the rest is history! After dating six years, we are now five years into our marriage, have two kids, and a whole bunch of love. Ladies and gents, Jeremy will tell a different version, but just know mine is the absolute truth, lol.

Jeremy

I met Brittany two times before our official introduction. It may not make sense on the surface when I say that Brittany and I interacted on three different occasions while only meeting formally once, so let me explain. I remember attending a Student Athletic Advisory Committee (SAAC) meeting one night on campus. Normally we had food at the meetings and at this particular meeting, there were tons of leftovers.

Since I was a college student through and through, you already know I had to take some leftovers with me. After the SAAC meeting, I headed to an FCA Bible study. At this point, our FCA organization was scarce when it came to the number of members that attended the meetings weekly. The only reliable attendees that came every week were a teammate of mine named Trevor, who was our campus leader for FCA, and me. We were dedicated and committed beyond convenience to Jesus and this organization.

I arrived at FCA that night, and to my surprise there was a young lady there, along with my teammate. They were sitting down, not in chairs, but on boxes that we athletes used to perform box jumps. I walked in and being a gentleman, I said hello to the young lady that I had never seen before. I politely asked her if she wanted any of the food I brought from my other meeting. This girl was Brittany, and she declined my polite gesture. Looking back at it, I know she only said no to the food because I was a stranger to her at the time, since contrary to what you may believe, Brittany really can eat. Do not tell her I said that, though.

How Brittany and I were seated in Bible study that night foreshadowed our future together; we just did not know it at the time. My teammate sat in the middle of us. Brittany resided on his left side facing him and I was seated on the right side facing him. My teammate is now a pastor, so looking back, that moment resembled our wedding ceremony that occurred six years later. At our wedding, we stood at the altar staring into each other's eyes, with a pastor in the middle facilitating our ceremonial union.

Brittany and I left that meeting and went back to our regular, scheduled everyday lives, which did not include each other. Then there was a Fall October day when Brittany and I had been led to attend another FCA Bible study on the same day. Speaking of being led, for those who are searching for and waiting for your future spouse to enter into your life, I suggest you seek God first and foremost. Do not go out every day, hunting for your spouse.

Instead, chase God and then He will lead you or guide you to being in the same setting, organization, or place that the spouse He has for you is present at. This is what God did for me and I know for so many others. At this point in my life, I was striving to grow more in my relationship with the Lord, which is why I continued to attend FCA Bible studies. When I attended the meeting, my goal was to learn more about God, but while being present at the meeting, I met my wife who was led to attend the Bible study due to her spiritual quest for God. So, ladies, Brittany met her husband while chasing God and the same can happen for you.

The Bible states specifically to men in Proverbs 18:22, "He who finds a wife, finds a good thing." When you first read this scripture, you can interpret it as, *I must go look for my wife, so I can find her.* However, I believe it can be viewed in another way. Have you ever been looking through your closet for a particular shirt and while you searched for the shirt, you end up finding a nice jacket or pants that would go with the shirt, even though that wasn't what you were originally looking for?

I believe the same goes when finding a wife. As we seek God, we stumble across and find the wife He has for us. It can be at a church event, sporting event, grocery store, or even a social gathering where you may find your wife. I did not go search for Brittany, but instead, I searched for God and subsequently found my wife. Ladies and gentlemen, when you let God guide you, then you run into your spouse, but when you try to find them on your own, then you may find someone and try to make them a spouse. There is a huge difference between the two.

At this October FCA meeting, Brittany shared her testimony about how she decided to commit to God by waiting to have sex until marriage. As she was testifying and displaying her gift of speaking and memorization by quoting scripture from the Bible, I sat in astonishment. I had never had the honor to witness a woman my age be as passionate about God and her relationship with the Lord as much as Brittany is, until that day.

Throughout the meeting, I remember glancing at Brittany's wedding finger while sitting in the meeting. I was not stalking her hand, but fellas, you know how we can do a ring check with our eyes. As I glanced at her hand, I saw that there was a gold ring on it. For some reason, I thought she may have been married or possibly engaged.

When the Bible study concluded, I wanted to tell Brittany how great she did, but I was too intimidated to do so. I chickened out and allowed her to exit the football facility and vanish into the night without uttering a word to her. Like *deja vu*, Brittany and I left that meeting and went about our lives, but this time we were on the same campus because Brittany had transferred from TSU to MTSU. I think she wanted to be closer to me, she just did not know it at the time.

I recall being single in my junior year of college and someone informing me that there was a great girl on campus who loved the Lord and who had decided to value her body and wait until marriage. I replied by saying that if it was meant to be, then one day, I would run into her and meet her. At this time, I did not know that the person informing me about this amazing girl was referring to the Brittany that I had seen in multiple FCA meetings. However, I was not going to run after a woman solely because she loved the Lord and decided to abstain from sex.

Those are remarkable qualities in a woman, and in fact, I did want those attributes to be in whomever I dated next. I had decided that just because a woman loves the Lord and is not having sex does not mean she is the one for me. Likewise for you, ladies, just because a man loves the Lord and is waiting for marriage does not mean he is for you. There are many Christian women and men in the world who choose to do that and guess what, all of those women are not for you fellas and all of those men aren't for you ladies.

There still has to be compatibility between you and that person. I know people who say, "Aw, man, I'm going after that person or this person because they are in the church or they are in the choir at the church." Those are the only qualifications that many people check for, but then you get involved with this person and you realize you and this person are not on the same level spiritually. That person may not have any problem partaking in premarital sex, drunkenness, or any habits that are sins in the eyes of the Lord. You find yourself confused and baffled because you thought they were different just because they went to church. Ladies and gentlemen, you cannot be fooled by that or incited to move hastily after a person solely because of their relationship with the Lord. Compatibility plays a gargantuan role as well.

Eventually, Brittany and I met officially, ironically at an FCA Bible study. We had a mutual friend, Ms. Erica, who informed both of us that the other one was going to attend FCA that upcoming week. I walked into that FCA meeting before Brittany arrived. When she finally came in, I went up to her and introduced myself.

I told her I had not seen her in a while. She immediately started crying. I cannot make this up. I asked her if she was okay and she said yes.

I thought I had hurt her feelings and I did not think she liked me after that. So, for the rest of the Bible study, I said nothing to her. After the Bible study, I told Ms. Erica that I did not believe Brittany liked me. I told her to give my number to Brittany.

We connected through text messages and became social media friends. I remember going through her pictures repeatedly to the point that one of my roommates said, "Man, J, you are feeling her." I replied by saying, "Yes I am!!!" I was enamored with her swag.

I could see her confidence protruding through the photos on the computer. We scheduled a first date with each other, which consisted of us going to, you guessed it, an FCA meeting and then out to the movies. I had to test her when she first rode in my Beamer (BMW) also known as a 2000 Saturn modeled car. I wanted to see if she was too religious for me or if I was not holy enough for her.

I believe in balance as a man of God and as a person. I will be honest—I listen to all types of music. I wanted to see if we were compatible in that area or would she judge me for not having Kirk Franklin playing in my CD player. So, I put on 2000's R&B and let it play.

As the song began to play, I noticed she liked the music. That was a revelation to me that not only were we in agreement with our faith, but we both were huge proponents of having balance in our lives. I courted Brittany the rest of the year and then Brittany and I became official in January 2010. I was her boyfriend and she was my girlfriend.

CHAPTER 4

WAITING DOESN'T ELIMINATE RELATIONSHIP AND SEXUAL BARRIERS

We enjoy watching podcasts, shows, and movies that deal with relationships, love, and marriage. As we were watching a movie, the topic of sex came up. The characters in the movie began to discuss how waiting until marriage to have sex could be misleading for some, which can lead to people being disappointed with their sex lives once they get married. After watching this movie, we knew we needed to address this matter in the book and offer our perspective on abstinence and married sex.

ABSTINENCE IS NOT THE CURE

Abstinence is not a cure for arguments. Choosing to wait does not prevent your relationship from experiencing any of the common growing pains that are ubiquitous in every relationship. Your significant other will still irritate you and do things that you wish they would stop. Your communication as a couple will still need to be worked on daily. There will still be imperative discussions about financial decisions, politics, spiritual stances, and goals, that you will need to have with your significant other.

Abstinence is not a cure for the sexual hurdles you may face. Whether you wait until marriage or you choose to indulge in fornication, there is a learning curve that comes with sex. Waiting does not make that learning curve disappear. When a man and woman have sex with each other, two people are coming together as one.

Now, the man has his preferences and the woman has her preferences. The man may have a particular way or position he enjoys, but the woman's favorite position may be contrary to his. That is okay as long as both work together to meet each other's needs and compromise with one another. This compromise and display of teamwork is required and must be done, regardless of whether or not the two people are married, for the experience to be fulfilling for both parties and not just for one.

If you are honest, then you can admit that you know way more about sex at your age now than you did when you were younger. Even more so, your sexual performance is a whole lot better now than it was in the past, especially if you are having sex with the same person. Even though we waited five years before we had sex with each other, there still were things we had to learn about each other sexually once we got married. We had to put in the same work to blossom the sexual intimacy of our relationship as someone who is not married does for their relationship.

THE ACT IS THE SAME; THE EMOTION IS DIFFERENT:

There may be a belief that married sex and out-of-wedlock sex are different. As it pertains to the actual act of sex, we believe it is the same. The human body does not change whether you are waiting or whether you are fornicating. The same sexual positions are afforded to someone married and someone single. Therefore, we as people should stop placing married sex, as it pertains to the physical act, on a pedestal. People should have a healthy and realistic perspective of what sex will be like for them once they are married.

Now, when it comes to the emotions of sex once you are married versus when you are single, we believe there is an extreme difference. We believe that there is a deeper emotional connection when you have sex with your spouse. This isn't just a random person from your job, or a person you met that night at a club, or even a significant other that you have been dating but there is no long-term or lifetime commitment made between the two of you. This is your spouse, to whom you said, "I do."

You are invested in this person and they are invested in you. You two have history. You two are a team and you're building an empire and a lasting legacy. Therefore, when such people come together to be intimate, it becomes deeper than just two people coming together for a sexual act. It's a spiritual connection, a soul connection, and a life connection. Your spouse becomes a part of you, and you are a part of them, and that taps into a depth of emotions that having sex with someone that is not your spouse most likely won't do.

Brittany

CHAPTER 5

LET'S TALK ABOUT SEX

Ladies, I believe on average, women tend to be more patient than men. But the truth is, women do not enjoy waiting either. We also would rather skip around waiting for things. When we arrive at the nail shop, the first thing we ask is, "How long is the wait?"

When we walk into the salon, the first thing that we ask is how many people are in front of us. The truth is, whether they are male or female, nobody enjoys waiting. Waiting takes discipline and dedication. It is never a fun thing to do, but it is the most rewarding thing to do.

Waiting helps you get the results that you were seeking. You are not rushing, you are not settling, but instead you are waiting to receive God's very best. That is exactly what waiting until marriage rewards you with. Sis and bro, it is time for us to wait on God's very best. There is no reason that we should have to rush into relationships that we know we should have never been in, just to have a relationship status on social media. My mom's favorite quote when I was growing up was, "Anything worth having is worth waiting for."

CONVERSATION WITH GOD

As I previously mentioned, I decided to travel to schools and share with ladies how I came to start practicing abstinence. When I met Jeremy, neither of us was a virgin. We were just two young people who came together with the decision to put God first in all that we said and did. I know God designed Jeremy for me.

The two of us were able to come together and agree that ultimately God designed for us to present our bodies as sacrifices. We both discussed how we knew in the past that we short-changed God and truly wanted to show Him how we could be obedient to what we knew was required of us. The decision to practice abstinence came from me being tired of being convicted. I was tired of living two lives. I was tired of giving in to sexual peer pressure.

I was tired of listening to my friends cry over the fact that they too had given a man something so special and he still managed to find other women to cheat with. I watched close friends become pregnant and ultimately still find themselves single. I realize things can happen even when you are married. But there is a high probability that you won't get married or that getting married may indeed happen at a slower rate, ladies, than you would like it to when you choose to have premarital sex. After watching friends and myself go through all sorts of turmoil, I decided it was time to stand for what I knew was right. It was time to dare to be different. It was time to strive to give God my best and wait on the best He had for me.

IT WORKED FOR US

When I was choosing to live what I call a double life, I would constantly cry to God because I knew that I was living in sin. I knew that I was sharing my body with someone who probably wasn't going to be my husband. I was constantly going back and forth with God on whether or not I wanted to wait. It was a constant repeat of me giving in to the peer pressure and me arriving at church repenting for what I had just done.

My conscience whooped me sore. Every time something didn't go right in my life, I wondered if it was because of how I was living. I know grace and mercy cannot be earned, but I was so afraid of the consequences of how I was living. Paul asked a very important question in Romans. He said, "Shall I continue in sin, that grace should abound?"

That is exactly what I asked myself. I remember sitting in my room on the floor, asking myself how long I was going to continue to live in sin and in return ask for forgiveness. I knew not only was I hurting my salvation, but I was also pulling someone along with me. I remember when I was living opposite of God's word, the guy I was dating at the time broke up with me when I told him I wanted to wait.

Everything in me told me that was going to happen. It was like giving someone a big gift and then deciding afterwards to take it back. That's exactly what I was trying to do. I wanted a gift back that I should have never given in the first place.

The scripture says "Whom He loves, He corrected." David said it best: "He chastened me many times, but He never gave me over to death." God has a way of getting your attention.

He is such a jealous God. He will not allow anything to stand in front of Him. He will remove it before He allows you to continually live a life opposite of what He has asked of you. God was constantly getting my attention.

He began shaking up situations around me, and more and more I began to feel myself become convicted. When you're young and you just keep running in the house, your parents then yell, "Stop, before you get a whooping." Well, that was me. I was afraid of the whooping. I knew the wages of sin were death and I didn't want the whooping. I did not want God to have to get my attention.

The great thing about God is that He will meet us where we are. Maybe you are like me, where you know you want to wait, but at the same time, you are scared to tell your significant other. Well, you can pray to God to give you the strength to be bold for Him. Maybe you are in a relationship and you love your significant other and you are honest enough to say you love having sex with them.

You are also honest enough to say you know that it is wrong and you want to give God more. Sometimes you have to pray to God and ask Him to protect you from yourself. We have to come to God and be honest with Him about where we are. He sees where we are, so you might as well keep it real. God loves us with flaws and all.

God can meet us where we are, but we have to first come to Him.

A Conversation with your Significant Other

I remember years ago when I told my boyfriend at the time that I was no longer going to engage in premarital sex. He told me that was the dumbest thing that he had ever heard. He told me there was no way he was going to be with someone that was practicing abstinence. He said everybody sins and reminded me that we were born into sin. I told him that I understood that I never was going to be sin-free, but I desired to sin less. I loved God too much and I wanted to save my body for the person that God designed for me to be with. His reaction let me know that it wasn't going to be him. I believed what my mom said.

The best things in life are worth waiting for. I knew that I was worth waiting for. I knew I was a gift and nobody besides my husband deserved the package. I may have feared being alone, but the fear I had for God was much stronger. I was so afraid to have that conversation with my ex, but there was no way I was going to continue to live my life like that.

I can't tell you that I have never failed or that I always get it right. I am nowhere near perfect. What I can tell you is that God truly will keep those that want to be kept. I wanted God to keep me, even if that meant keeping me from myself.

By me acknowledging to God where I was, He was truly able to meet me there. God can meet us where we are, but we have to first confess our sins to Him. At that time in my life, I wondered if God had decided that I would be single forever. I began thinking there was no way that I was going to find a man who was going to practice abstinence. Although all types of fears ran through my mind, I was determined to go ahead and tell my ex that I couldn't live my life like that anymore.

Ladies, this is where many of you sit in your life; you are at the crossroads of doing what God wants or doing what your man wants. Fellas, many of you are at the crossroads of doing what God has called you to do or going along with what your friends are doing. I can only tell you what truly worked for me. The truth is that a little step of obedience years ago led me to grow and it led me to be with the person God designed for me to be with.

You never know what God is up to, but He truly is always doing more than we imagined. That conversation, that I mustered up the courage to have with my significant other, led me to whom God was preparing me for. The man God designed for me did not have the sole goal of getting my body. Do not get it twisted. Jeremy and I wanted to make love to each other.

We just knew we were going to have to do what God wanted and then what we wanted in God's timing. There's nothing more rewarding than walking in obedience and God then giving you your heart's desires. That's exactly how it happened. I gave Him something fake in my life and in return He gave me something real.

When I met Jeremy, I had no clue he was going to be the one who was going to decide that I was worth waiting for. What I will say is that I'm glad that I was up front with Jeremy about what I didn't want to do. He let me know that we were in this together and that we were going to struggle together. As you continue reading, you will find out how.

Isaiah 59:2 states, "But your iniquities have separated you from your God; your sins have hidden his face from you so that he will not hear." The scripture tells us that sin separates us from Christ. Every day we are striving to be more like God. Although we make mistakes daily, that does not mean we should just sin and ask for forgiveness. That is ultimately taking advantage of God's grace. Each day we put our best foot forward and try to take the necessary steps to live a life pleasing to God. You cannot hear from God and be distracted at the same time.

If you ask my husband, he will tell you I cannot text and talk at the same time. I will either lose track of thinking, start texting what I'm saying, or not even hear you. Multi-tasking is a weakness of mine (lol). I'm getting better, but I have learned that I can't do both things at the same time. That's how it is with God! You cannot say you love Him but care more about pleasing your significant other.

You cannot do both. How can you hear what God is saying to you and be distracted by your flesh? I do not think you would wait to tell someone something important while you were at a football game. Why? Chances are, it is way too loud at the football game for you to hear and it would be more suitable to converse in a more private setting. So, why do we try to seek God and live the way our flesh wants to at the same time? God is a jealous God and needs your undivided attention.

Maybe you are thinking, *Well, Brittany and Jeremy, I haven't developed a relationship with Christ yet. I have heard about Him, but I don't know Him for myself yet.* You might be wondering how you can hear from someone that you don't yet know. All you have to do is invite Him in. Let Him know what areas you want Him to work on with you and He will.

Jeremy

In high school, my friends and I would always talk about sports, television shows, music, and of course, the ladies. When girls became the topic of discussion, our conversations were never about abstinence or what we were not trying to do with the girls. It was contrary to that. My friends and I were not disrespectful to women in our colloquies, but with much excitement, we disclosed to each other what we did, were doing, or attempting to do with the girls. Being celibate was something we could not even fathom at that point in our lives. Sadly to say, abstinence is no more at the forefront of most adult men's minds than it was when they were boys. Perhaps it may be further removed from their minds now because sex has been prevalent in their lifestyle from adolescence to well into their adulthood.

Fellas, I understand who we are as men. I am not declaring that to abstain from sex you must turn off your radar towards women you perceive to be beautiful or attractive. I acknowledge that whether married or single, you will always notice gorgeous women, but how you talk about them and what you do when you see those women should change with your maturity as a man, boyfriend, fiancé, and as a husband. I am honest with other men and I let them know that we all see the menu (women) when we are out and about, whether it be on a college campus, in church, or at the mall, but we can decide to not order from the menu.

You do not have to talk to her because she is pretty. There is no need for you to get every lady's number that you perceive to be your type. For the majority of men, our interactions with each other typically never consist of conversations about waiting until marriage. I believe when we transition into being adult men and being in dating relationships, out of respect we typically do not ask other men that we know if they are having sex with their significant other. We kind of assume that they are sexually active with their girlfriend or fiancée. Usually, as men, if we ever have a conversation about abstinence in our lifetime it will probably be initiated by someone or something else. Hopefully, this book can be a conversation starter for you as it pertains to you abstaining from sex until marriage.

CONVERSATION WITH GOD

The first real conversation I had about waiting until marriage was with God. Yes, I remember being in church and hearing how God wants us to save our bodies for marriage. My parents expressed this to me as well, but it was not until I began to partake in premarital sex that I truly began hearing God talk to me as it pertained to sex.

When I first began fornicating, I thought I was having fun. I knew I was wrong, but still, I continued to do it. As months and years passed, the conviction from the Lord commenced speaking louder to me. After I would finish having sex I would then be overwhelmed with guilt.

God repeatedly told me, "You are wrong, Jeremy." He said, "You need to stop what you are doing and practice abstinence." I began to reply to God and express to him how I felt about everything. I would ask God to help me avoid the results, consequences, and outcomes that could potentially arise after fornicating. I would pray for forgiveness, even though I knew I was going to go and repeatedly make the same ill-advised decision to fornicate. Despite repeatedly fornicating, I did know that if I kept testing God and playing with fire, then eventually God would let me fall flat on my face instead of extending grace to me time after time. I knowingly did wrong by partaking in premarital sex. I eventually listened to God and decided to heed His advice in the conversations He was having with me.

Some of you have been hearing a little voice that's been probing you to wait until marriage. You are realizing that sleeping with a woman or women who are not your wife, let alone even your girlfriend, is not as fun anymore. Some of you are trying to figure out why you are getting that feeling of conviction before or after you partake in sex. There are a few of you though, who are thinking, *I do not hear a small voice, nor do I feel conviction.*

In fact, you are still having the time of your life, floating from woman to woman or just being intimate with that same woman who is not your wife. Maybe this is not you either, but what about you guys who have babies with women that you are not with anymore? Consequently, a percentage of your check may be going towards paying child support. How about those who have had to go to the doctor because they have received an STD? If this is you, then I need you to comprehend that this is God attempting to get your attention and have a conversation with you. He is trying to caution you that you need to stop what you are doing and do it His way, which is to wait until marriage. I harken you fellas to relinquish what you are doing and offer God your undivided attention while simultaneously being receptive to His message.

HAVING A CONVERSATION WITH YOUR SIGNIFICANT OTHER

Through continuous conversation with God, I realized that I not only was having conversations with Him about abstinence, but I was now bringing the conversation to the woman I was talking to at the time. As men, when we have decided to adhere to God's instruction, then we must be bold enough to have these conversations with the women in our dating life. I must admit that on two separate occasions I failed in executing abstinence after initially expressing to women that I wanted to wait until marriage or stating to them that I was not trying to go to that particular level of intimacy with them. After having conversations like this, I still found myself succumbing to the temptation, thus fornicating with them.

What I realized, though, is that it is not about just having conversations with any woman you are dating or involved with, but you must have these conversations with the right woman, or else you will find your conversation to be unproductive. Consequently, you and that woman likely will fall into fornication.

When I say the right woman, I mean a woman who has committed to God, in her own life, to wait until marriage. In my errors as a man, I take full responsibility. No woman made me do anything that I did not want to do. I realize where I fell short. I did not put myself in situations or relationships that were conducive to sexual purity. Spiritually, I was at the point of wanting to wait until marriage, but my flesh was not all the way there.

I tried to have conversations with women who spiritually had not committed to saving their bodies until marriage, and obviously, their flesh desired it as well. As humans, we all have the fleshly desire to have sex. Therefore, as men, we need to internalize the notion that the women we talk to desire to have sex as well. Though this is the case, we must realize that sex is a bonus. Sex is the icing on the cake. The cake itself and what's most important is who she is as a person. Knowing what's in her heart is key.

I decided in my heart that I wanted to practice abstinence. I expressed this to women who in their hearts had not committed to abstinence. In their hearts, they were okay with premarital sex. It is a bad combination, fellas, when you desire in your heart to practice abstinence, but you choose to get involved with women whose hearts are okay with sex before marriage. Due to the fight against fleshly desires being so difficult, it's even more vital for you two to be on the same page spiritually about waiting.

To win the battle against fornication, it takes a commitment spiritually from the man and woman. The commitment from the man represents the right hand of a boxer and the commitment from the woman represents the left hand of a boxer. A boxer can win a fight with two strong hands, but if that boxer breaks his hand during the fight and then has the use of only one, then that boxer probably will lose. If you attempt to practice abstinence with a woman who lacks the spiritual commitment to waiting— which then means you are fighting against fornication with one hand—then fellas, you will find yourself failing and having sex as I did.

As a man, if you have not decided in your heart that you are going to wait until marriage, but you try to date a woman who has, one of two things will usually happen. You either will tempt that woman enough to where she gives in and has sex with you, or you two probably won't work out because she does not want to compromise her faith, morals, and commitment to God and abstinence. Trying to refrain from sex in your own strength typically does not work. You need the woman you are dating to be fighting with you and not against you.

The same applies to the man. You both should be working towards remaining abstinent, instead of one wanting purity and the other one being okay if sex is a part of the relationship. Amos 3:3 KJV says, "Can two walk together, except they be agreed?" You and the woman must be of one accord.

Fellas, some of you are with women now that you know if you were to bring the idea to her that you wanted to practice abstinence in your relationship until marriage, she would flip out and refuse to do so. You know that abstinence would help your relationship because this is what God desires for you to do among many other things in your relationship, and it would bring blessings to you both because you would be walking in obedience. These are tough conversations to have with your significant other, but they must be had. One thing you can do is pray to God that He touches her heart and allows her to have a change of heart and be receptive to what you are saying.

As I encourage you to pray for your significant other to be on the same page as you, I also want to warn you about trying to be Captain Save'em. A good friend told me once that you cannot change a person. Therefore, make sure you are not compromising your morals and relationship with God by staying with someone and continuing to fornicate. You do not need to continue to converse, date, associate, or interact with a woman that you know is not on the same page as you are when it comes to being sexually pure until marriage.

CHAPTER 6

I'M NOT TRYING TO HEAR IT

SHE WANTS YOU TO WAIT

F ellas, some of you are in a relationship right now and you and your girlfriend or fiancée have been intimate with each other already. You have been dating for some time and now she has sat you down to have a conversation with you. In this conversation, she has expressed to you how much she loves you and how much she wants to spend the rest of her life with you. Then suddenly she changes the tone of the conversation.

She musters up enough courage to inform you that she has decided to wait and wants you both as a couple to wait until marriage. On the other hand, there are some of you who are single, and you just met a young lady. You have gone on a couple of dates with her and you believe she is the one. You go on a date together, and while out eating, she utters to you that she is not having sex before marriage.

Fellas, what do you do when your woman or a woman you are interested in brings this to you in conversation? Do you pass up on a great woman because you refuse to wait? Is sex more important to you than the type of person she is? Would you acquiescently agree to be with a different woman who will offer her body to you without a marital commitment despite her not measuring up to the caliber of person your girlfriend or fiancée is?

My brothers, we've got to see deeper than the extrinsic factors. True intimacy consists of sex, but as a married man, I have been taught by my wife that intimacy is multifaceted and much more than the sexual act. The woman you are in a relationship with has way more to offer you than her body. A woman's body may keep your attention for a moment, but the intangibles that make up who she is will keep you focused and in love with her forever. Therefore, ask yourself, men, how much is premarital sex worth to you? Is it worth giving up your soulmate for a temporary situation?

QUALITY TIME > SEX

We know sex is very important to any marriage. With that being said, most of your time as a couple will be spent having quality time with each other. That quality time consists of talking, watching television, brainstorming for your businesses, traveling, and hanging with the kids. If all you do is have sex before being married, you may struggle to master the art of spending quality time with your spouse.

It appears that when you are not supposed to do a particular thing, then that is when you want to do it all the time. As we've already indicated, God desires for us to wait until marriage. Even though this is God's desire, there is a great temptation to ignore that and choose to not wait. It is similar to telling a kid that they could play with any toy, but they cannot play with the iron.

That child will gravitate towards playing with the iron because they were told not to. If you habitually do more fornicating with your significant other than anything else, then how much harder will it be for you to develop the skills needed to spend quality time once you two become married? When you get married, there are different factors that can come into play and interfere with your sex life, but those factors will not hinder the quality time you spend with your spouse if you do not let it. There will be times your spouse is too emotionally spent to have sex; maybe there is a physical issue that could be preventing you and your spouse from making love; or maybe the kids are being blockers and will not go to sleep. As a result, you and your spouse have to put on hold the physical act of intimacy and instead hold each other's hand as the kids jump from couch to couch. Whatever the case may be, just know that you and your spouse will need to know how to spend effective and efficient quality time with each other.

We believe that placing sex on the back burner and waiting until marriage will in return cultivate your ability as a couple to excel in the area of spending quality time together. Many people utter the phrase "Ever since we got married, we do not have sex as much." But God never intended His people to have this belief or experience, because we were not supposed to have sex before marriage. If you wait, then you will not have anything to compare your sex life to. However, we understand that you may have not waited.

We did not wait either as it pertains to the grand scheme of sex before marriage, but we waited for each other, and as a result, once we got married, we could not say to each other, "Hey, we used to have way more sex when we were just dating." If we made love five times a week or if it was one time, we learned that this is what sex as a married couple is like. Sometimes you make love frequently and there are times you may not. But we know that spending quality time with one another will feed our relationship and keep it growing strong.

Brittany

HE WANTS YOU TO WAIT

Ladies, I know each of you are at different places in your life. Some of you are single, waiting on Mr. Right; some of you are in relationships; and some of you have never given a thought to waiting. Ladies, the man God has truly designed for you wants you to wait. How do I know? Because the man God designed for you to be with cares about when He opens the package.

When you give people Christmas presents, why don't you give them to the person on December 1st? When someone's birthday is in February, why don't you give them their birthday gift in January? You do not operate in that manner because you do not see the point in giving them their gift early. It is special to the person when you give them their gift on that special day.

I remember getting Jeremy a new pair of shoes around December 10th one year. I went ahead and let Jeremy get them and put them on. Now in my head, they were for Christmas. In Jeremy's head, because I gave him the shoes early, they were just a gift. He wasn't counting it as a Christmas gift. Ladies, have you been sharing your gift? As a result, the man you are sharing this gift with believes that it is just a gift. See, ladies, the reason Jeremy didn't think the gift was for Christmas was because I gave him the present early. There was no surprise, it was not wrapped, I just said here you go and handed it to him. Jeremy wanted a present to unwrap and he wanted it on Christmas.

The man God designed for you may indeed want the gift early, but at the same time, he really doesn't want to open the gift early. He wants to be surprised and he wants to unwrap the gift on the wedding night. Let's be real, you couldn't wait for Christmas to open your gifts. But although you may have wanted to open your gifts early, you didn't. It's perfectly human to want to, but you have to decide if you are going to.

I remember in college, talking to my cousin and asking him, "When you get married, how do you want your wife to be?" He said, "I want my wife to be like a brand-new car. I don't want her to have a lot of scratches, looking like she is used. I don't want her to have a lot of miles as if she has been passed from owner to owner."

He said, "I want my wife like a brand-new car." That's what I desired to be for my husband. I wanted to be a brand-new car. God said, in 2 Corinthians 5:17, "Therefore, if anyone is in Christ, the new creation has come: The old has gone, the new is here!" Sis, you can still be a new car to your husband. You are just going to first have to confess your sins to your Father.

1 Corinthians 6:19 (NIV): "Do you not know that your bodies are temples of the Holy Spirit, who is in you, whom you have received from God? You are not your own."

CHAPTER 7

WHAT'S IN IT FOR ME?

The two of us knew that the road of waiting until marriage was going to be a difficult one. We were not unrealistic when it came to our expectations. We took our time and got to know one another. We got to know each other's strengths and weaknesses. We got acquainted with each other's flaws and all.

There was a time when Brittany asked her mom the question, "How does one know if the person they are dating is the person they are supposed to marry?" Her mom responded by saying, "You know it is the person when you can accept them just as they are." Meaning that if this person didn't change a thing, you could live with it.

It doesn't mean that you would not want your significant other to change in areas, but that you can accept who they already are. We were able to fall in love with who we are as people and not what tricks we could do in bed with each other. It was not just a physical attraction but an emotional connection.

There was a post on Facebook and a girl stated that there was no way she was going to wait until marriage. Now, we understand to each their own. We are not your parents, nor are we your God. We are only telling you what worked for us, as well as telling you what God requires.

The young lady went on to say that you must test drive the car before you buy it. Listen, when you purchase a car, you get 14 days to return it. If anything is wrong with the car once you make the purchase, you can then send it back for a full refund. The problem with us test driving with our bodies is that once you drive the car, there is no refund. You have given the person something that you cannot get back and that is a piece of who you are.

When we were dating, we trusted that God was going to match us with someone who possessed the same sex drive, and give us the ability to fulfill each other's sexual desires. We both knew what we desired out of the spouse we would marry. You know, when you buy a house, you do not get to move in first. When you order your food, you do not get to eat half of it and then decide not to pay for it. That is what the two of us decided to do. We decided to buy the product first and trusted God that it would work.

We understand that each of us has different conviction levels. So, in areas that we may struggle with, you may not. There is not a grey area in what God says about waiting until marriage. We believe that people often create a grey area in their heads.

They say things like, "Well, at least this is my boyfriend/girlfriend." They go on to say that waiting until marriage is only for people who are sleeping with more than one person. One of our favorite lines we've heard is that waiting until marriage is only for people who are not engaged. In whatever way we can, we will find a way to make the choices that we make sound better. Whatever your reason may be, just know there are many benefits to choosing to wait until marriage.

IMPROVED COMMUNICATION

Intimacy and sex are a form of communication between a man and a woman. When you are in the act of sex, you are communicating to your spouse that you love them, you appreciate them, you want them to feel good, and maybe you are even saying you're sorry through these actions. However, many times this form of communication is substituted for verbal communication, which we believe is okay to do at times, in a healthy marriage. Unfortunately, many times sex is the primary form of communication and may even be the only type of communication in a relationship among men and women who are only dating, engaged, or just friends. Using sex as your go -to form of communication can rob you of truly developing the skills that you must possess to verbally resolve the issues that rear their ugly heads in your relationship.

With sex being obsolete in our dating and engaged relationship, it allowed us to focus on our communication. If we offended each other, then the only way to resolve the issue was to verbalize how we felt. There was no kissing on each other trying to get the other one in the mood to distract each other from the real issue at hand. There was no rushing each other to hurry up and express what we were feeling about our relationship, or what was going on at work, or the personal goals we have, just so we could get to the bedroom and make love. Over time, we learned to sit and listen to each other with the intent to understand and not just respond. We have not completely mastered communication, but the precedent that we set for our communication while waiting and dating has fared us very well in our marriage.

CLEAR DECISION MAKING

Keeping sex out of the picture of your relationship as you date allows everything to be exposed. The good and the bad comes to light. When you first start dating, both you and your person of interest are putting on a partial façade. You both are pretending to be flawless.

Some of you may be saying, "Well, I do not want the bad to come to light in my relationship," but you need it to. You need to know what you can or cannot deal with in your relationship before proceeding to marriage. However, so many times sex covers up concerning issues. You tolerate issues that are deal breakers for you because of how that person makes you feel sexually.

You express to your friends that this person disrespects you all the time, but you follow that up by stating that the sex is awesome, so you stay. Or you declare to yourself, "I do not feel like a priority in this person's life, but they make me feel so special when we are intimate." As a result, you remain in the relationship. By doing this, you let the sex become a masking agent, but when sex is not included, you confront issues with clear judgment.

BRITTANY AND JEREMY KELLEM

If you feel repeatedly disrespected, then you should remove yourself from the situation. Sex in a non-marital relationship can serve as beer goggles. You are liable to run into all types of problems when your vision is impaired by sex. Remove the sex until you are married, so you can see and think clearly.

NO PRESSURE

Anyone that has ever been in a relationship can attest to the fact that the more titles you add to a relationship, the greater the pressure and expectations are. The world attempts to condition us to live by checkpoints when we're in a relationship. We are told that we should be kissing after a certain amount of time. After time has elapsed, the two of you should then engage in sex.

Then once you add sex into the equation, now you should consider moving in with the person. According to the world, it is cost-friendly to combine two mortgages into one. Yeah right, that's only a justification to move in with someone you barely know and is not your spouse.

The pressure we are referring to many times does not come from the world, but is intrinsic and comes from within. You may consider having sex with the person you are with because you know they have needs that they want to be met. Subsequently, you struggle back and forth on whether you should do it because you fear that the person may leave and find someone else if you withhold sex from them. Maybe the expectations are being placed upon you by neither the world nor yourself, but by your significant other. Your other half begins begging you to engage in premarital sex with them. They express to you that you both have been together too long to not take the next step in the relationship.

For us, waiting granted us the opportunity to dodge these forms of pressure and expectations. We both had an understanding that there was only so far physically our relationship was going to go before we were married. The standard was set from day one, so there was no confusion about what was or could happen in our relationship. When you enter a friendship or relationship with open-ended expectations, you leave yourself vulnerable and susceptible to compromising your values and standards.

As humans, we are good at expressing to someone "Hey, I just want to be friends who hang together and chill and nothing more." This expectation can sometimes be interpreted by the other person in many ways, which can result in things becoming way more than you ever intended them to be. We advise you to be clear with what you expect and hold true to it. If you make the stance to wait until marriage and the person you are entertaining is attempting to cross that invisible sex boundary, then that is a clear indicator that you need to leave that person, because they do not respect your wishes.

LOVE BUILT ON THE RIGHT FOUNDATION

If someone were to ask you if you love your significant other or your fiancé, you would probably say yes. That is great, but this follow-up question that we are about to ask may be more important than the first question. What is the love for the person you are with rooted in? This is a question that many people don't take the time to self-assess and find out the true answer.

When you partake in premarital sex, there is a tendency that your love for a person can be determined by how that person physically makes you feel. In other words, your love for your significant other likely is rooted in what they could do for you or physically offer you. On the contrary, when you remove sex and superficial things from a relationship, then your love can grow deeper and be centered on who that person is on the inside. When you wait and fall in love, you are falling in love with that person's personality, character, and intangibles, which is a stronger foundation to build your love for a person on. When your love for a person is centered around these key pillars and not sex, then your relationship will prove to be healthier and stronger to deal with the challenges of being in a relationship. Sex should enhance your existing love for a person. Sex shouldn't be why you love that person.

HELPS YOU GET TO KNOW YOUR SIGNIFICANT OTHER

Before they met, Brittany was interested in being with a man who was going to first lead her spiritually, then emotionally, and once they got married, then he would be able to lead her physically. Jeremy understood and began to lead her spiritually by praying with her, reading the Bible with her, and through his actions towards her. Jeremy led Brittany emotionally by showing her that he wanted something other than just her body. He showed her that he wanted her mind. His actions revealed that he cared about the things that Brittany cared about and was concerned about the things that bothered her.

Once we started dating, we decided to wait until marriage. That did not mean we became perfect people. We still had daily struggles. There were still things we were working to become better at and of course there were still areas we fell short at. Just to be transparent with you, we wanted to have sex. When we were dating, we desired to be with each other intimately. Meeting each other was a dream come true and the human part of us wanted to act on those feelings. So, it wasn't that we did not want to do it, it was that we knew we wanted more out of our relationship.

We wanted to show that even as young adults we could control our actions. Ultimately, God controls everything we do, but He allows us to make choices. We were choosing the healthiest choice, which was to wait. We were able to strengthen our communication, fight fair, and even grow together spiritually.

Waiting taught us a lot about ourselves. It allowed us to learn and see from past relationships that sex doesn't solve problems. If sex solved problems, we're sure the divorce rate would not be so high. If sex solved problems, people would still be with their "first."

Oftentimes people will use sex to solve their arguments. It doesn't solve the argument; it just makes the problem go away for the moment. It's more like a quick fix. Quick fixes do not strengthen the relationship and won't make a marriage last. We had to learn from each other as boyfriend and girlfriend.

Then when we got married, we had to learn about each other as spouses. By waiting to have sex, we were able to take our time and get to know each other without having sex clouding our thinking. We did not overlook little things that we wanted the other one to get better at. We were able to have constructive conversations to discuss with each other the things we could work on.

You may hear married couples all the time complaining about things the other person has always done. How are you going to complain to someone about something you never said anything about in the past? Could it be that the sex clouded your judgment? You have married that person and now you are trying to reprogram their way of doing things.

SELF-CONTROL

One of the areas of our lives that we grew the most in after waiting until marriage was the ability to demonstrate self-control. One may believe they have self-control, but ask them to go without sex for an extended period of time and then you will see if they possess it. If you have ever fasted from eating, then you can attest to how difficult that is. See, when you are fasting, you are not just fighting against your desires of wanting to eat, but you are going against the physiological requirement of your body needing to eat.

The same is true with sex. Yes, we have a desire to have sex, but we also have been created by God to possess hormones and a sex drive. God has commanded us to be fruitful and multiply as long as it is in the context of marriage between a man and a woman. Therefore, in our being, we want to have sex, so choosing to wait is choosing to fast from sex. Take it from us, being able to abstain from sex for a substantial amount of time will strengthen your ability to exercise self-control.

Our self-control was refined through the practice of abstinence, but we see the benefit of having that quality in other areas of our lives. For instance, we learned how to feed our spirit and starve our flesh. One of the things we have worked on in our spiritual life is being slow to speak. We are learning that everything does not need a response and we do not have to let every little thing become a big thing.

By practicing self-control, you take command of your actions. You then realize that you can determine the healthiest outcome and make clear decisions. There is nothing more gratifying than making clear choices. Self-control equals clear choices.

Think about it! You know how when you are so hungry you grab that Snickers bar to hold you over until your next meal? Then after you eat that Snickers, you are upset with yourself because you spoiled your dinner. On top of that, maybe you are trying to lose weight and tone up, but you just couldn't wait until you got your dinner.

Have you ever been in a rush to buy some new shoes as soon as you saw them in the store? You just had to have those new shoes and you knew you were going to be too fresh in them. Only to get home and see the store sent you a coupon, or worse, two days later, the shoes have gone on sale. You then realize you did not have to buy those shoes when you did; you could have exercised self-control and waited. Practicing abstinence will develop you in the area of self-control and possessing self-control will pay dividends in many areas of your life.

CHAPTER 8

WAITING & DATING

In the earlier chapters of this book, we have emphasized getting to the decision of practicing abstinence. With that being said, let's just say that you, the reader, have decided to wait until marriage. You have talked with God, yourself, friends, or your significant other and you have committed to abstinence until marriage in your life and relationship. You and your significant other are now waiting and dating. Deciding to practice abstinence is one thing, but we know thriving in the lifestyle of abstinence is an entirely different challenge.

So many times in life, a person will tell you how to reach a level of success, but they fail to equip you with the information you need so you can sustain the success once you arrive at your destination. We remember growing up and being told ad nauseam to graduate from college and everything would be okay. What society forgot to mention was what to do with the college degree or how to make the degree work for us. We do not want to simply encourage you to make it to a specific point, only to then fail you by not supplying you with the tools needed to help you succeed once you arrive there.

We have already told you what abstinence is and why we did it, but now for the biggest question there is: how did we do it? We used to get that question all of the time. People just couldn't understand why we were doing it, let alone how we were doing it. Honestly, we look back and ask ourselves the same thing. How on earth did we wait for so long? Nobody likes to wait, especially when you know what you are waiting for.

In this chapter, we want to supply you with practical information that we found to be useful for us as we waited and dated. We are not saying these are the only options that will result in successfully abstaining from sex until marriage, but we know these have proved to be beneficial for us and we believe they can and will be beneficial for you as well.

ASK FOR HELP DAILY

If you are going to be able to wait and date, the first thing you must grasp is that you cannot do it alone. You are a human and there is a battle going on within you. Your flesh does not want to wait, but your heart and spirit want to. To keep this battle under control and ensure your heart and spirit win, we believe you must cry out to the Lord for help daily.

You have to go to God and let Him know the areas where you are weak. Be honest with God and take off the facade when you come to Him. So often we want to come to God when we have it all together, but God wants to meet us at the altar just as we are. God can't fix what we are not honest about that we are dealing with. We had to ask God for help to get enough courage to practice abstinence and we had to ask God to help us abstain once we started.

At times when you feel as though you are struggling to pray, you can seek Godly counsel. Reach out to a mentor or someone that goes to your church. Let them know the areas you are struggling with and ask them to pray with you. The scripture mentions "where two or three are gathered, He shall be in the midst."

You may wonder if we literally asked God to protect us from having premarital sex. The answer is yes. We prayed that He would protect us. We prayed for Him to keep us from our selfish temptations.

We prayed that God would help us learn to love ourselves more than pleasing each other. We prayed that God would help us put Him first in all we say and do. To be more transparent with you, we prayed on the nights we were weak, that we would be strong enough to remember that we were worth waiting for. We remember asking God for help and guidance on how to wait and date.

We prayed consistently throughout the dating and engagement portion of our relationship, asking God to keep us as we strove to be Christ-like in our waiting. We felt like Paul in the second part of Romans 7:18: "For I have the desire to do what is good, but I cannot carry it out." Many of you feel the same way. You are repeatedly telling yourself, "I want to wait; I want to do the right thing with my significant other," but you feel compelled to submit to the temptation of sex. We advise you to call on the Lord for supernatural help, because you cannot do this alone in the natural world.

GUARD YOUR MIND

You must protect your mind. It is so important to watch what you let enter your mind, because if you are allowing inappropriate things inside your mind, then it will make it much more difficult to successfully wait and date. You may be trying to figure out what we mean by protecting your mind. You may be asking what it means to protect your mind and how to do it. Well, allow us to articulate what we mean.

We as humans can ask God to be our helmet of salvation and to protect our minds, but we must do our part as well. Vain images, ideas, and thoughts enter our minds through our senses. Consequently, what we hear, see, or touch can infiltrate our minds and harm us spiritually, mentally, emotionally, psychologically, and in other ways. This can prove to be a hindrance to you on your quest to wait until marriage.

To guard your mind, you must be truthful about what you can or cannot handle. We will be transparent and share something we individually had to do to help ourselves out as we practiced abstinence. Jeremy chose to stop going on the explore page of a specific social media site after a certain time of the day. The explore page went from being pictures of families, businesses, and funny videos to a page full of women in bathing suits or provocative clothing.

At first, Jeremy tried to convince himself there was nothing wrong with just looking at pictures. *They are only pictures, right?* he thought. Wrong! They are more than pictures.

We believe that seeing things that are sexual can arouse your sexual desires and place images in your head that you do not want there. Therefore, Jeremy knew that he had to stop feeding his mind that. Viewing those pictures was not going to make it easier for Jeremy to refrain from fornication and he wanted to make sure he did not build a habit of looking at things like that because that's a slippery slope. Even though we weren't married yet, Jeremy made up his mind that "the buck stops here." He did not want to bring into the marriage an unhealthy habit of viewing inappropriate things, which could be detrimental to a marriage sexually and as a whole.

We now want you to think about what it is that you need to stop feeding your mind. Is it that television show, maybe a particular song, or maybe the strip club? But whatever it is, you must come to the point where you make up in your mind that you are done. There must be a decision made by you that whatever unhealthy thing you feed your mind that has control of you must be omitted from your life.

We will keep it one hundred with you. You probably will not go cold turkey overnight from whatever your vice is. It wasn't at the snap of a finger that Jeremy stopped going on the explore page after a specific time, but with a lot of asking God for help, like we mentioned before, along with establishing self-discipline, Jeremy then was able to refrain from feeding his mind those unhealthy images.

Once again, remember it's all a process, ladies and gentlemen. Instead of normally watching that show every day, you cut back and may watch it three days a week. From three days to one and from one to none. Therefore, do not get discouraged if you have not erased that out of your life, completely, as fast as you would like to, but don't be proud either that you are still doing it, because the goal is to not do it at all. Furthermore, know that you are working towards that goal of sinning less and less and feeding your mind less and less garbage that can be contradicting to the lifestyle of abstinence you wish to live until marriage.

When extracting the negative images and habits out of your mind, you must replace them with positive things. I know for us when things come to our minds that aren't of Christ or anything we want to think about, we strive to cast them down. We admit that we need to be more consistent with doing it. What we mean by casting down is when sexual thoughts come to your mind that you do not want to be there, we want you to know that you possess the power to cast down the thought by speaking the Word of God.

You can recite to that thought the scripture 1 Corinthians 2:16: "I have been given the mind of Christ," or you can reply to the thought by stating the scripture Isaiah 54:17: "No weapon formed against you (me) shall prosper." It may sound unorthodox to you when it comes to trying it, but we believe and know that it does work. Changing the television station of your mind and filling it with things of Christ and positivity is very beneficial.

We have learned through our journey that some things that cross our mind are not thoughts of our own and do not always need to be addressed. Ladies, if you see an attractive man, or fellas, if you see an attractive woman, you do not need to endorse the way he or she looks by uttering words that highlight their attractiveness. When you do this, you have activated a thought and brought it to life. Beware of doing this because thoughts can turn into words, words can then turn into actions, and that is a slippery slope.

WEDDING DAY AS A MOTIVATOR

Like any tough challenge, obstacle, or strenuous task in life, to persevere and accomplish a goal, you must possess motivation. What if someone asked the question, "What motivates you to stick to abstinence until marriage?" The spiritual answer is so you can walk in obedience and please God. This was true for us, but what motivated us just as much was our wedding day.

There were stretches where we were super frustrated about waiting and dating, even to the point we wanted to give in at times. We would then focus on how special our wedding night was going to be as a way to inspire us to keep pressing through these emotions and maintain an abstinent lifestyle. We even discussed the possibility of forgoing our commitment to abstinence and God, and instead choosing to indulge in fornication. After considering it, we would quickly return to our senses and then express to one another how much it would dampen our excitement for the wedding day if we chose to fornicate with one another.

We know, ladies and gentleman, that the wedding day is not solely about sex. But let's be real—we know that when the pastor states in jubilation that you are now husband and wife, the idea of making love to each other immediately jumps to the forefront of a couple's minds. The wedding day is like Christmas. Christmas is not solely about receiving gifts, but we still wake up expecting to receive something from our significant other.

Romans 12:2 (NIV): "Do not conform to the pattern of this world, but be transformed by the renewing of your mind. Then you will be able to test and approve what God's will is– his good, pleasing and perfect will."

CHAPTER 9

PLAYING WITH FIRE

DON'T PLAY WITH FIRE

Whether you are in a relationship or single, you should refrain from playing with fire, or else you will be burned. Trust us, we know from first-hand experience. What we are referring to when we say fire are the situations between men and women that can cause them to stumble and break their commitment of abstinence.

We know that everyone is different when it comes to specific weaknesses when dealing with the opposite sex. Some of us can handle watching a movie with a person, cuddled up with the lights off, and nothing goes down. The two of you just only watch the movie. Then some people can stay the night over at their significant other's place, or their significant other comes over to theirs, and it does not lead to sexual intimacy.

What about the man who can go on a date with a woman while she is wearing a sexy dress, or the woman who can go to dinner with a guy who is sporting a nice, fitted blazer along with a pleasant smelling cologne, and still maintain the strength to resist fornication? We could go on and on, but the bottom line is that as people, we must be honest with ourselves and admit what makes us weak. If we are not truthful to ourselves, then we walk in arrogance as we have before. Learn from us. Jeremy has admittedly placed himself in situations, before he and Brittany met, that he thought he could control himself in, only to find out that the situation got too hot for him, and as a result, he ended up fornicating. What began as a chill session went further than it really should have.

Ladies and gents, even when you are strong in areas, if you expose yourself to continual temptation, you can then weaken yourself to the point where you give in. It is similar to a strong, tall tree. If you were to take one swing at it with an ax, the tree would not fall. Even after taking ten good hacks at it, the tree may still be standing. However, as you get north of 20 attempts, the tree begins to lean because it has been weakened and consequently it falls.

Ladies and gents, you are like that tree. You start strong when you and your significant other cuddle up to watch a movie with the lights off. You resist the first time. Then the next time you watch a movie, you cuddle a little closer and you two kiss, but nothing else transpires. Two weeks pass and you both agree to another movie night.

This particular night you begin cuddling, but you are kissing throughout the entire movie. Hands are beginning to get a little frisky and before you know it, clothes begin to come off, but before you two go the distance, you stop each other. You make it through the night without having sex, but you have become that once strong tree that is now leaning. You may have considered yourself strong enough to endure the temptation that comes with cuddling and watching a movie with your significant other, but we need you to remember this:

If anything or anyone is subjected to a substantial number of repetitive blows from a formidable object, then that thing will eventually cripple and cave in. Always know that you are no different when it comes to temptation. God will always provide a way out from temptation (1 Cor 10:13), but the more you intentionally put yourself in the face of temptation, the more difficult it will prove to be to choose the way of escape that God provides.

Ladies and gents, please remember to evaluate yourself and realize when you have become that leaning tree. Acknowledge when you have become so weak that you know if you watch a movie with your significant other one more time, it is going down, and we are not referring to the Young Joc song. When you are honest with where you are, then you take the necessary precautions to avoid succumbing to the temptation. Do not attempt to be a superwoman or a macho man and decide to see how many blows from temptation you can take and still remain standing. You do not know your limit until it is too late and you have already passed it.

Ladies and gents, once you are honest with yourself about your weakness, you then must be honest with your significant other. We were honest with each other in the dating aspect of our relationship. Brittany recalls when she would become turned on to Jeremy if he hugged her in a certain way. There were times when we knew it was only because of God that we had not given in to our sexual desires.

We used to tease each other that we were sexually frustrated. At the end of the day, we knew we were making the right decision. Like we stated before, there were some steamy times throughout our dating relationship where we wanted to give in to the temptation and have sex with each other. Thank the Lord He kept us from giving in, even though we wanted to. However, we walked away from those situations repenting of our sin and understanding what led us to the point where we almost broke our commitment.

We expressed to each other how we needed to avoid doing specific things because of what they lead to, or we can't do *that* because we know those particular things lead to us wanting to have sex with each other even more. Know the buttons within your relationship that you need to avoid pushing so you can avoid dabbling in premarital sex. Remember, the more you avoid putting yourself in compromising situations, the better chance you and your significant other have at waiting until marriage.

When you reminisce about being a kid, you can remember all the talks your parents had with you; it's not until later that you begin applying it to your own life. Brittany remembers when she was a little girl, her mom used to tell her all the time, "If you taste the appetizer, then you are going to want the full meal." How often have you eaten the appetizer and then were so full that you didn't want the meal? Now, occasionally that may happen, but on average it doesn't.

Most of the time you taste the appetizer and then you still want the full course meal. That's how sexual flirtation can be. You taste a little sample and then you want more. Our advice is simple, ladies and gents: don't play with fire.

You know as well as we do, you can't be spending the night all the time at each other's place and think it's not about to go down. Trust us, we know. We had to learn our limits and establish our boundaries too. We had to stop playing with fire because we didn't want to get burned.

CHAPTER 10

THE STRUGGLE IS REAL

We knew we wanted to keep it 100% about the journey of abstinence. We want you to know that if you choose to embark on the journey, it will be challenging. It is real. We want you to comprehend that abstaining from sex when you are single and abstaining from sex while in a relationship are both difficult, but they present different obstacles.

Being single can be when you feel the most liberated in the sense that you believe that all your choices and actions only affect you. You are not obligated to another person. You are free to date, talk to, or sleep with as many people as possible. You think you can lie down with a person one night and wake up the next morning and go on with your life as if nothing ever transpired. Daily you are on the prowl for the next beautiful or most attractive person to add to your list. It may seem that simple, ladies and gentlemen, but it is much more complex than that.

God created us to not be alone. Most men and women want to have a companion, but you do not want the commitment that is ubiquitous in any monogamous relationship. Consequently, you cultivate a horrible habit. Single men and women, we warn you that developing the habit of fornicating is dangerous. Once you start, it is hard to stop. We know because it was difficult for us. So, it is best to wait until marriage to start having sex—that way, you will be able to satisfy your sexual urges and demands with your spouse in a sexually pure way. However, we know there are so many that did not wait to experience sex, including us.

When we go around having sex with people who aren't our spouses, we set a precedent in our lives where we expect to get sex from our significant other or an acquaintance without a vow or obligation. Subsequently, for many of us, when we encounter someone of the opposite sex, we immediately have our hands out. Some people do not want friendship, conversation, or a relationship with another person. They sometimes want to bypass all of that and hop in bed with the person.

This type of conceptualization gets etched deeper into your ideology the more premarital sexual encounters you have with someone who is not your spouse, and even more so, not even your significant other. If we are not careful, we can find ourselves accepting this behavior. You can get accustomed to this way of life and that may lessen your desire to ever want to be married and or be in a serious relationship. Many people ask themselves, "Why should I be in a relationship with a person when I can receive marital benefits from them even though they are not my spouse?" If you let them, most people will not buy the cow if they can just get the milk instead. We advise you to do your best to refrain from sampling the milk prematurely so that the entire cow will be worth buying. We are not comparing humans to cows, but you get the point.

To those who are in a serious monogamous relationship and even engaged, premarital sex presents harm to you as well. How do we know? Well, we have been in relationships where we were not pure, and we realized the side effects it had on us. When you are in a relationship and are having sex, you can tend to think you are better than others who are single and fornicating.

You may justify what you are doing by saying, "At least I'm having sex with the person that I am in a relationship with." This makes no sense. It is like thief number one saying that they are not as bad as thief number two because thief number two robbed a bank and thief number one only robbed a convenience store. Wrong is wrong. Both are thieves, and whether you are having sex in a relationship, with a friend, or with a stranger, you are still considered sexually impure by God because they are not your spouse.

Abstaining while in a relationship is like choosing to fast from sweets while they are within your reach. We acknowledge that it is laborious to resist eating sweets even if they are not in your presence or not stocked in your cupboards in the kitchen. However, we want you to imagine how challenging it would be to resist sweets when there is a sweet potato pie in the refrigerator and a bowl of candy sitting on the kitchen table. Every time you stroll through the kitchen, the temptation to eat candy or pie is at an all-time high because you can see, smell, and touch the sweets. That's exactly how it is when abstaining from sex while in a relationship. Every day you see this beautiful woman or handsome man, you appreciate the inner beauty that God has given them. You spend countless hours with this person, being able to see them, smell them, hold their hands, and kiss them, but God still expects you not to cross the forbidden line.

Even though we knew that the temptation to have sex with each other was going to increase considerably once we became an official couple, we still elected to keep our relationship absent of sex. Lord knows, though, that the choice we wanted to make was to be able to make love to one another. We were attracted to each other spiritually, mentally, and physically, so if it were up to us, sex would have been prevalent in our relationship as we dated, but it was our commitment to God that made us do otherwise.

Hopefully by now, there has been something that we have said that has triggered you into considering waiting until marriage. One of the things that everyone hates is when you purchase something, and people don't tell you how hard it is to put it together or how much work it will be when you take it home. Well, we will not sell you a dream and make this look easy. It is not the hardest thing to do in life, but it is surely not the easiest thing to do either. We vowed to keep it real with you and let you know that the struggle is real.

We knew God had called us to give Him more and we understood the importance of honoring Him with our bodies. We can only tell you from personal experience that it will be worth it. We knew God wanted to teach us how to find a lifetime of happiness with someone and not just temporary lustful moments. The two of us will both tell you that while growing up in church, we learned why we should practice abstinence, but we weren't told how hard it might be.

Throughout the time that we were practicing abstinence, God spoke to us about obedience being better than sacrifice. People would probably say that it is much easier for a woman to practice waiting until marriage than it is for a man. They will say that women are more concerned with keeping their body counts lower from the fear of being labeled certain things. Maybe women are concerned with their body count, but women also want to have sex and desire to please their spouse.

No matter what, whether you are a man or a woman, even the thought of celibacy can be extremely hard. We knew in our hearts that we didn't want anything to block our blessings nor delay them. We wanted the things that God planned for us. It's not that we didn't want to have sex, because Lord knows we did. We just knew that sex was not worth trading our peace, joy, or our happiness.

Maybe you are saying to yourself, *Well, I like sex and I do not know if I can fully give it up until marriage.* Hey, thanks for the honesty. Yes, you may indeed like sex, but do you like it enough to disappoint God? Do you like it enough for it to be a gift that you give everybody, and it becomes nothing special for your spouse?

Do you like it enough for unwanted diseases or unplanned pregnancies? Do you like it enough to cost you your blessings? We doubt you do. Although this might be the hard thing to do, it is the best thing to do.

CHAPTER 11

ALL THINGS ARE MADE NEW

After everything we have expressed thus far in this book, some of you are still saying to yourself, *Well, I am not a virgin,* or *I already have been sexually active with my significant other, so I'm not looking forward to the wedding day as much because I know what it is like*—either to have sex, period, or more specifically, to have sex with your significant other. Well, let us debunk that way of thinking. We were not sexually active with each other before marriage, but we were not virgins. We knew what sex was like. However, we kid you not, ladies and gentlemen, God has the power to make all things new. The scripture Revelation 21:5 reminds us of God's ability to do so.

As we progressed in the waiting and dating stage of our relationship, we perceived each other as being new, pure, and simply like a virgin. Our past did not matter. We were moving forward with a new perspective on each other—a Godly perspective. Believe it or not, this can happen to you and your significant other.

It matters not what you have done in the past with someone else or with each other, God can have you motivated to abstain and be excited about being able to make love to your spouse on that wedding day as if it were your first time being with each other. Remember, it is never too late for you and your significant other to wait until marriage. Do not believe the lie that says since you both have been sexually active with each other, or since you are not a virgin, you might as well continue to have premarital sex. Always remember this: God is a God of second, third, fourth, and so on chances.

Perspective is key when it comes to perceiving yourself as being made new. Think about this. When you go to buy a car, many times it is not a brand-new car that has never been driven. Much of the time, it is a used car that some previous owner already has driven and decided to trade in after owning it for some years.

Now you, the person who goes to buy the used car, perceive that car as being NEW, despite the miles, the scratches, and the damage that may have been done to the car. You leave with the belief that you have a new car. That is the same thing God can do for you. No matter the people you have slept with, no matter the damage that has been done to you or you have done to others, and no matter how many times you may have slept with your significant other.

God can send you someone who will only see you as a new car, or if you are in a relationship, God can have you and your significant other begin to look at each other with fresh eyes and a new perspective on the relationship. So please hear us again when we say that it is never too late to decide to wait until marriage. No matter if you are single in college, or if you are dating in your mid-20s, or even if you are engaged in your 30s, 40s, or 50s, the benefits of waiting are available and long-lasting for everyone who chooses that way.

CHAPTER 12

HE IS TEACHING YOU HOW TO WAIT IN OTHER AREAS

We know that throughout our book we have expressed to you that waiting will be beneficial to your spiritual life and dating relationship. However, the benefits of waiting to have sex spill over into other aspects of your life as well. Waiting as it pertains to sex is probably one of the hardest things you can do in life. We laugh and joke about it now, but during that season there was nothing entreatingly funny about it. Waiting produces discipline that you can utilize when you have to wait in other areas.

All of us can attest that we have had to wait for something. We can all agree that waiting has never been fun nor entertaining. What we can say is that there have been things in our lives that were worth the wait. Think about your dream job. You went through not-so-good jobs and now you are working with purpose and doing what you were created to do.

You can now appreciate your dream job, due to all the other jobs that did not work out. There are levels in every walk of life. Maybe you are at your dream job, but you are not in your dream position. There are some things in life that you must wait for.

Maybe you have come to your job and were hired for an entry-level position. After hard work and dedication, you will get a promotion. It is a must that you stay the course and wait on it. Maybe you are waiting for your dream house.

Make sure that you are taking the necessary steps for God to grant you the things that you are praying for. That may mean building your credit or paying down some debt. If it is making some wise financial choices, make sure you make them. Waiting and preparing are two key ingredients to crushing goals and getting the things you want out of life.

WAITING VS. SITTING

There is a difference between waiting and sitting. When someone says that they are waiting on the doctor or waiting for the food, they really are sitting rather than waiting. Waiting involves preparing. So, if someone says, "I am waiting on an opportunity," that person is preparing themselves for the opportunity.

That opportunity may come a year from now, a month from now, a week from now, or it may come tomorrow. However long the opportunity may tarry, that person in the meantime is reading books, studying, practicing, and developing their skills so that when the opportunity arrives, they will be able to handle it and thrive in it. This applies to waiting until marriage to have sex. While you wait, it is not a chance to waste time. As you wait, you must develop as a person and as a couple. Whether you and your significant other wait five years or a month before you are married, be sure to develop the character and foundation of your relationship. The time spent waiting should be used to prepare yourself for the weight of sex in a relationship.

Sex is amazing, but it is not to be taken lightly. Responsibility, expectations, and other things come with sex. If sex is introduced too early in a relationship it can stifle the growth and development of the relationship and ultimately cause it to come to ruins. That is why the waiting period must be used wisely.

The waiting period should be used to get to know each other as people, of course, but also how you think or operate when it comes to different things that come up in a relationship. The waiting period allows you to see if you and your significant other are compatible. Do your personalities click? Are you both dream-oriented? Do you both have similar ideas about parenting?

Do you both want kids and at what age? How do you both respond to adversity or conflict? Do you have congruent views of how finances should be handled? Do you like their family? Where would you two like to settle down and live? What are your future goals and aspirations and are they cohesive with the other person's dreams?

We can go on and on, but these are some things that, during the waiting period, you should be establishing as a couple because these things are important. If sex is brought into the relationship too early, then sex can cause a couple to table these topics for a later discussion—one that they don't have until it's too late and they're married. Now you are trying to figure out how you overlooked the fact that you and your significant other have two different spiritual views or two different ways of parenting the kids. Well, we can help you with the answer. You probably were blinded by the sex.

The thing that we as humans do is underestimate the power and weight of sex. It's like seeing a bag on a floor that appears to not weigh a lot. We approach this weight nonchalantly and with the wrong mindset. We believe that this bag is so light that we can pick it up in any type of way.

So, as we bend down to pick up the bag, we lack the proper form that is required to pick up a bag of this weight. As a result, we pick up the bag and immediately find out the heaviness, but it's too late. We've injured ourselves because we lacked the proper form and foundation that would protect us and enable us to lift and carry a bag of this size without suffering an injury. That is how we as humans treat sex.

We say, "Oh it's just sex." Therefore, we approach it, or we attempt to add it to our relationship before the relationship is stable or before the relationship even has a sturdy enough foundation to have sex be a part of it. There is a reason why God wants sex to come after marriage. God knows how great it is, but He also knows the power and complexity of it.

A school system would never put an eight-year-old in 12th grade because the student is not prepared for that level of work. Likewise, sex can be considered 12th-grade work and you and your significant other may be in third grade as it pertains to the maturity level and character of your relationship. Therefore, why would you want to add sex into your relationship at this point if you haven't been through the waiting process, or prepared yourself for the level of work that automatically comes with sex as it is added to a relationship?

A FRIENDLY REMINDER

We want to close by reiterating that waiting is not a punishment, but it is a time of preparation for you as an individual and for you and your significant other to take advantage of, so that you two are equipped and ready to thrive in all facets of your relationship while waiting and dating until you both say I do.

The scripture states,

"For the vision is yet for an appointed time; But at the end it will speak, and it will not lie. Though it tarries, wait for it." - Habakkuk 2:3

www.ingramcontent.com/pod-product-compliance
Lightning Source LLC
Chambersburg PA
CBHW060251030426
42335CB00014B/1651